The National Trust Book of

NATURE
POEMS

T0025987

The National Trust Book of

NATURE
POEMS

TREASURED CLASSICS
AND NEW FAVOURITES

Edited by Deborah Alma

 **National Trust**

Published by National Trust Books
An imprint of HarperCollins Publishers
1 London Bridge Street
London SE1 9GF
www.harpercollins.co.uk

HarperCollins Publishers
Macken House, 39/40 Mayor Street Upper,
Dublin 1, D01 C9W8, Ireland

First published 2023

ISBN 978-0-00-859602-6
10 9 8 7 6 5 4 3 2 1

A catalogue record for this book is available from the British Library.

Printed and bound in the United Arab Emirates

If you would like to comment on any aspect of this book, please
contact us at the above address or national.trust@harpercollins.co.uk

National Trust publications are available at National Trust shops or
online at nationaltrustbooks.co.uk

This book is produced from independently certified FSC™ paper
to ensure responsible forest management.

For more information visit: www.harpercollins.co.uk/green

Contents

Introduction

The first ever anthology of verse was published in 1557, and contains the poem 'Soote Season' ('sweet season') by Henry Howard, Earl of Surrey:

The soote season, that bud and bloom forth brings
With green hath clad the hill and eke the vale;
The nightingale with feathers new she sings;
And turtle to her make hath told her tale.
Summer is come, for every spray now springs;
The hart hath hung his old head on the pale;
The buck in brake his winter coat he flings;
The fishes flete with new repairèd scale;
The adder all her slough away she slings;
The swift swallow pursueth the flies small;
The busy bee her honey now she mings;
Winter is worn that was the flowers' bale.
And thus I see among these pleasant things
Each care decays, and yet my sorrow springs.

British poets have long had a special connection with nature, and poetry has reflected our changing relationship with the natural world. As in Howard's poem, matters such as the rising of the sap in spring and its promise of new life and renewal have inspired many of our best poets. We have a strong history and culture of nature poetry.

Some of the poems in this book reflect a growing despair at how we treat our natural world, and the natural world, in turn, is often used in poetry to express anxieties and states of mind – it can be cruel, benevolent, remote, familiar, or strange. Sometimes the poet is there, immersed in nature, at the heart of the poem, and sometimes they feel shut out or are merely an observer. But many of the poems come from a place of faith that nature will always recover and endure – a traditional lyrical response to the external world, held up as a mirror for the poet's psyche or for humankind more widely. My intended emphasis in this anthology stems from my own work of writing and well-being, putting together a collection that sees the natural world as an antidote to times when the 'world is too much with us', as Wordsworth so beautifully puts it. These are poems that serve for a moment to take us, at least in our minds, outside. The book contains seven chapters, each of which explores a different aspect of nature.

Often 'nature poetry' conjures up the male Romantic poets, and there are plenty of those represented here, but I hope too that you'll find a range of both established and lesser-known contemporary poets, with their diverse voices and ways of seeing the natural world. But still, but still…there were so many beautiful and well-known poems that I didn't have the space to include, and in compiling the book I had terrible moments of waking up early in the morning thinking, 'oh no, there are no poems of polecats… or robins…or…'. I apologise if your favourite poems are missing. It was an agony of exclusion. Pity the anthologist!

Some of the poems or poets in this book are linked in some way to National Trust sites or have been inspired by them. Where this is the case, there are notes on pp. 154–155 explaining the connection.

I hope that this book will bring a little of the wildness and weather into your sitting rooms and bedrooms. I hope, too, that as well as inspiring you to explore nature with more of a poet's eye, paying attention more imaginatively and philosophically, it will also encourage you to seek out more of the works of the poets included.

The Changing Seasons

The poems in this chapter observe, respond to and marvel at the seasons' signs and shifts and the mercurial changes in the weather. There is nothing quite so British as our relationship with the weather. We are drawn to its very changeability, its meanings and memories, and the way it touches and transforms the natural world.

If ever world were blessed, now it is.

(from 'April Rise' by Laurie Lee)

Thaw

Over the land freckled with snow half-thawed
The speculating rooks at their nests cawed
And saw from elm-tops, delicate as flowers of grass,
What we below could not see, Winter pass.

Edward Thomas

(1878–1917)

Spring

Nothing is so beautiful as Spring –
    When weeds, in wheels, shoot long and lovely and lush;
    Thrush's eggs look little low heavens, and thrush
Through the echoing timber does so rinse and wring
The ear, it strikes like lightnings to hear him sing;
    The glassy peartree leaves and blooms, they brush
    The descending blue; that blue is all in a rush
With richness; the racing lambs too have fair their fling.

What is all this juice and all this joy?
    A strain of the earth's sweet being in the beginning
In Eden garden. – Have, get, before it cloy,
    Before it cloud, Christ, lord, and sour with sinning,
Innocent mind and Mayday in girl and boy,
    Most, O maid's child, thy choice and worthy the winning.

Gerard Manley Hopkins

(1844–1889)

But These Things Also

But these things also are Spring's –
On banks by the roadside the grass
Long-dead that is greyer now
Than all the Winter it was;

The shell of a little snail bleached
In the grass; chip of flint, and mite
Of chalk; and the small birds' dung
In splashes of purest white:

All the white things a man mistakes
For earliest violets
Who seeks through Winter's ruins
Something to pay Winter's debts,

While the North blows, and starling flocks
By chattering on and on
Keep their spirits up in the mist,
And Spring's here, Winter's not gone.

Edward Thomas

(1878–1917)

I So Liked Spring

I so liked Spring last year
    Because you were here; –
    The thrushes too –
Because it was these you so liked to hear –
    I so liked you.

    This year's a different thing, –
    I'll not think of you.
But I'll like the Spring because it is simply Spring
    As the thrushes do.

Charlotte Mew

(1869–1928)

Home-Thoughts, from Abroad

Oh, to be in England
Now that April's there,
And whoever wakes in England
Sees, some morning, unaware,
That the lowest boughs and the brushwood sheaf
Round the elm-tree bole are in tiny leaf,
While the chaffinch sings on the orchard bough
In England—now!

And after April, when May follows,
And the whitethroat builds, and all the swallows!
Hark, where my blossomed pear-tree in the hedge
Leans to the field and scatters on the clover
Blossoms and dewdrops—at the bent spray's edge—
That's the wise thrush; he sings each song twice over,
Lest you should think he never could recapture
The first fine careless rapture!
And though the fields look rough with hoary dew,
All will be gay when noontide wakes anew
The buttercups, the little children's dower
—Far brighter than this gaudy melon-flower!

Robert Browning

(1812–1889)

April

machine of spring with all your levers thrown to max
clouds in ripped clothes and sheep trailing afterbirth
where last week's buds sucked blue juice from the dusk
now the branch is swollen   priapic
cherry bling and hawthorn sex-bed smell
motorway hedgerows on thrust   electric rapefields

your levers are jammed and nothing can pull them back
not now   not frost   not squall
city gutters clogged with blossom
muddy ponds spuming with cannibal tadpoles
the long blinding days   your bashed clock
the violent small hours   magpie clacking at the robin's nest

and us lying open-eyed all night
breathing in the white noise of pollen
hearing the long bones of the trees stretch and crack
wondering   will you ever power down or is this it now
wondering   what can any death among us mean to you
and will we make it through to summer or is this it now

Jean Sprackland

(1962–)

On a Lane in Spring

A Little Lane, the brook runs close beside
And spangles in the sunshine while the fish glide swiftly by
And hedges leafing with the green spring tide
From out their greenery the old birds fly
And chirp and whistle in the morning sun
The pilewort glitters 'neath the pale blue sky
The little robin has its nest begun
And grass green linnets round the bushes fly
How Mild the Spring Comes in; the daisy buds
Lift up their golden blossoms to the sky
How lovely are the pingles and the woods
Here a beetle runs; and there a fly
Rests on the Arum leaf in bottle green
And all the Spring in this Sweet lane is seen

John Clare

(1793–1864)

April Rise

If ever I saw blessing in the air
I see it now in this still early day
Where lemon-green the vaporous morning drips
Wet sunlight on the powder of my eye.

Blown bubble-film of blue, the sky wraps round
Weeds of warm light whose every root and rod
Splutters with soapy green, and all the world
Sweats with the bead of summer in its bud.

If ever I heard blessing it is there
Where birds in trees that shoals and shadows are
Splash with their hidden wings and drops of sound
Break on my ears their crests of throbbing air.

Pure in the haze the emerald sun dilates,
The lips of sparrows milk the mossy stones,
While white as water by the lake a girl
Swims her green hand among the gathered swans.

Now, as the almond burns its smoking wick,
Dropping small flames to light the candled grass;
Now, as my low blood scales its second chance,
If ever world were blessed, now it is.

Laurie Lee

(1914–1997)

Wrack of Summer

All along the lake shore the brambles
are coming ripe, swelling, shiny

compound eyes as traffic mirrors.
In the water red beech leaves turn

with each wave. Light ticks away
disguised as wasp drone. The fringes are fraying.

Red leaves in the water. Brown leaves on the shore.
The wrack of summer.

The trees are still full of it. Bracken
high and green. It feels like a trick

if you expect one thing
to not be so much like another.

In the water I drift. Red leaf
pretending I could still be green,

A damselfly, May-blue, skims by.
We are all as confused as each other.

If we stop moving, we come to ground.
Brown leaves on grey stones. The wrack

of summer. All along the lake road
things dying, or coming into their own.

Polly Atkin

(1980–)

Looking Down On Glen Canisp

The summer air is thick, is wads
that muffle the hill burn's voice
and stifle colours
to their cloudier selves – and
bright enough: the little loch
is the one clear pane
in a stained-glass window.

The scent of thyme and bog myrtle
is so thick
one listens for it, as though it might be
a drowsy honey-hum In the heavy air.

Even the ravens
have sunk into the sandstone cliffs
of Suilven, that are dazed blue
and fuzz into the air around them –
as my mind does, till I hear
a thin far clatter and
look down to where two stags
canter across the ford, splashing up before them
antlers of water.

Norman MacCaig

(1910–1996)

Adlestrop

Yes, I remember Adlestrop—
The name, because one afternoon
Of heat the express-train drew up there
Unwontedly. It was late June.

The steam hissed. Someone cleared his throat.
No one left and no one came
On the bare platform. What I saw
Was Adlestrop—only the name

And willows, willow-herb, and grass,
And meadowsweet, and haycocks dry,
No whit less still and lonely fair
Than the high cloudlets in the sky.

And for that minute a blackbird sang
Close by, and round him, mistier,
Farther and farther, all the birds
Of Oxfordshire and Gloucestershire.

Edward Thomas

(1878–1917)

Who Has Seen the Wind?

Who has seen the wind?
Neither I nor you:
But when the leaves hang trembling,
The wind is passing through.

Who has seen the wind?
Neither you nor I:
But when the trees bow down their heads,
The wind is passing by.

Christina Rossetti

(1830–1894)

On the First Day of Autumn

I give myself permission
to go outside
so nature can have a different look
and a different sound

a different sound in the stream
running over stones

a different look
in the floor of yellow leaves
of autumn just begun

I allow myself to listen
to have rest
in squirrels that run above my head

On the first day of autumn
I think about a tree   uprooted
and thrown down   that has sent
some of its roots back down into the ground

walking my mind in the dug-out road
of this tree   in its bole
of rotting leaves

this is the farthest I have come
to the edge of the world

a human walking on a tree
hanging my mind from the tussling odours
of mulch bark and rain

from a latticework of limbs
and roots exposed in a hanging grimace

This is the farthest I have come
to the edge of the world
to the edge of the work of
making the land home

so land
can have a different look and
a different sound

not of angry dogs and knives
but the sound of
my feet pressing down
into the flesh of the leaves

Jason Allen-Paisant

(1980–)

To Autumn

Season of mists and mellow fruitfulness,
　　Close bosom-friend of the maturing sun;
Conspiring with him how to load and bless
　　With fruit the vines that round the thatch-eves run;
To bend with apples the moss'd cottage-trees,
　　And fill all fruit with ripeness to the core;
　　　　To swell the gourd, and plump the hazel shells
　　With a sweet kernel; to set budding more,
And still more, later flowers for the bees,
Until they think warm days will never cease,
　　　　For summer has o'er-brimm'd their clammy cells.

Who hath not seen thee oft amid thy store?
　　Sometimes whoever seeks abroad may find
Thee sitting careless on a granary floor,
　　Thy hair soft-lifted by the winnowing wind;
Or on a half-reap'd furrow sound asleep,
　　Drows'd with the fume of poppies, while thy hook
　　　　Spares the next swath and all its twined flowers:
And sometimes like a gleaner thou dost keep
　　Steady thy laden head across a brook;
　　Or by a cyder-press, with patient look,
　　　　Thou watchest the last oozings hours by hours.

Where are the songs of spring? Ay, Where are they?
　　Think not of them, thou hast thy music too,—
While barred clouds bloom the soft-dying day,
　　And touch the stubble-plains with rosy hue;
Then in a wailful choir the small gnats mourn
　　Among the river sallows, borne aloft

Or sinking as the light wind lives or dies;
And full-grown lambs loud bleat from hilly bourn;
Hedge-crickets sing; and now with treble soft
The red-breast whistles from a garden-croft;
And gathering swallows twitter in the skies.

John Keats

(1795–1821)

Something Told the Wild Geese

Something told the wild geese
It was time to go.
Though the fields lay golden
Something whispered,—'Snow.'
Leaves were green and stirring,
Berries, luster-glossed,
But beneath warm feathers
Something cautioned,—'Frost.'
All the sagging orchards
Steamed with amber spice,
But each wild breast stiffened
At remembered ice.
Something told the wild geese
It was time to fly,—
Summer sun was on their wings,
Winter in their cry.

Rachel Field

(1894–1942)

The Rainy Day

The day is cold, and dark, and dreary;
It rains, and the wind is never weary;
The vine still clings to the mouldering wall,
But at every gust the dead leaves fall,
    And the day is dark and dreary.

My life is cold, and dark, and dreary;
It rains, and the wind is never weary;
My thoughts still cling to the mouldering Past,
But the hopes of youth fall thick in the blast,
    And the days are dark and dreary.

Be still, sad heart! and cease repining;
Behind the clouds is the sun still shining;
Thy fate is the common fate of all,
Into each life some rain must fall,
    Some days must be dark and dreary.

Henry Wadsworth Longfellow

(1807–1882)

The Unlooked-for Season

Love, the sun lies warm along the wall.
The wide windows and the smell of the road
Do not say 'Winter.' Ladybirds are crawling
Out on ledges. Midday full on the land
Slows down the progress of the afternoon
Promising evening, like a Summer Sunday.

But look where the sun is. Never high in the sky
It crept around the horizon. Ask anyone,
Look at the trees and the calendar – all declare
It should be Winter. Within two hours
The Winter night will come up with the fog.

Since you have come and gone in the dreaded season
And left so much in sunlight, I cannot think
Of now as a dead time, only gentle,
With nothing to be feared, of this is Winter.

Jenny Joseph

(1932–2018)

The Year's Midnight

The flown, the fallen,
the golden ones,
the deciduous dead, all gone
to ground, to dust, to sand,
borne on the shoulders of the wind.

Listen! They are whispering
now while the world talks,
and the ice melts,
and the seas rise.
Look at the trees!

Every leaf-scar is a bud
expecting a future.
The earth speaks in parables.
The burning bush. The rainbow.
Promises. Promises.

Gillian Clarke

(1937–)

February on Reservoir Hill

Anthills are sealed against frost and wind.
The moon has slipped tethers of brown grass
and rises early through cloudless blue.

A bullfinch flushes the hawthorn gap
but his mate whistles him back to the south slope
where buds will open first.

Down in the housing estate a starling ruffles
up sunset and churrs into the north wind
seeking the rest of its roost-bound flock.

Chris Kinsey

(1956–)

Animal Life

In these poems, the poet's eye roams across the landscape and does what poetry does best. It stops to look carefully and exactly, and to celebrate what is seen and felt – from the purpose and fury in a snail's determined nighttime hunt, to the mysteries of the mud-shrimp, and the secret thoughts of the stag.

a fox in her fox-fur
stepping across
the grass in her black gloves
barked at my house

(from 'Fox' by Alice Oswald)

Pied Beauty

Glory be to God for dappled things –
   For skies of couple-colour as a brinded cow;
     For rose-moles all in stipple upon trout that swim;
Fresh-firecoal chestnut-falls; finches' wings;
   Landscape plotted and pieced – fold, fallow, and plough;
     And áll trádes, their gear and tackle and trim.

All things counter, original, spare, strange;
   Whatever is fickle, freckled (who knows how?)
     With swift, slow; sweet, sour; adazzle, dim;
He fathers-forth whose beauty is past change:
          Praise him.

Gerard Manley Hopkins

(1844–1889)

Considering the Snail

The snail pushes through a green
night, for the grass is heavy
with water and meets over
the bright path he makes, where rain
has darkened the earth's dark. He
moves in a wood of desire,

pale antlers barely stirring
as he hunts. I cannot tell
what power is at work, drenched there
with purpose, knowing nothing.
What is a snail's fury? All
I think is that if later

I parted the blades above
the tunnel and saw the thin
trail of broken white across
litter, I would never have
imagined the slow passion
to that deliberate progress.

Thom Gunn

(1929–2004)

Hunting the Stag

The stag doesn't visit because you want him to. It doesn't work like that.
He doesn't materialise when you go out to look for him
with the good camera this time, coiled around your neck
and your sheepskin hat with the ear flaps on.
He does not trot down from the hill to greet you, tamed by your need.
He has his own matters to attend to. What did you expect?
You know what you become when you're like this. Too much, too much.
Scanning for movement in the undergrowth, beady and atavistic.
When you press your palm on the stone gate post and wish your wish
is selfish. The heron passes asking *what are you missing when you only look
for big things?* A selfish wish never comes good.

He is higher than you can walk today, or deeper.
You cannot make him come to you.
Not the great stag with his rustling mane not even
the small roe with his sapling antlers.

He will be standing in the shadow of the side street when you lock
up the shop. He will be standing in the shadow of the house
when you stay out too long, talking on the path through the trees
about loss till the fells dissolve into dusk and push you down to him.
You will feel him before you hear him.
You will hear him before you see him.
He will seem to step out of the walls of your house
or through them. You will think he is waiting for you
but you are incidental. He will go
to a place you haven't worked for years,
wade into the lake, bristling as swans
ripple out from his image. Don't want so much.

Come down from the woods. Empty your pockets
of pinecones and sticks. Light the fire. It doesn't work like that.
Light the candles. Nothing does.

Polly Atkin

(1980–)

Brown Hare

Amberswood SD 6065003727

All hail the hare, the strength of her stillness –
the muscle and fire in the length of her haunches –
a flare from the long grass – all power, all ear –
racing and boxing, half-mad with desire!

Let's hear it for hare – outgunning the car,
outrunning the farmer, rapid as river,
swifter than motorway, bumper-to-bumper –
quicker than progress and fleeter than fear –

flushed out and hunted by poacher and hunger,
the bullet and buzzard, the lurcher and lamper –
the truth of the hare, here in muscle and amber –
in the flame of her eye – still burning, still running

back to old Lancashire, back to the grasses –
a million or more running faster than foxes
back over centuries, back to the mosses –
dear quarry rewriting her story – all glory!

Clare Shaw

(1972–)

The Names of the Hare

(from the Middle English)

The man the hare has met
will never be the better of it
except he lay down on the land
what he carries in his hand –
be it staff or be it bow –
and bless him with his elbow
and come out with this litany
with devotion and sincerity
to speak the praises of the hare.
Then the man will better fare.

'The hare, call him scotart,
big-fellow, bouchart,
the O'Hare, the jumper,
the rascal, the racer.

Beat-the-pad, white-face,
funk-the-ditch, shit-ass.

The wimount, the messer,
the skidaddler, the nibbler,
the ill-met, the slabber.

The quick-scut, the dew-flirt,
the grass-biter, the goibert,
the home-late, the do-the-dirt.

The starer, the wood-cat,
the purblind, the furze cat,
the skulker, the bleary-eyed,

the wall-eyed, the glance-aside
and also the hedge-springer.

The stubble-stag, the long lugs,
the stook-deer, the frisky legs,
the wild one, the skipper,
the hug-the-ground, the lurker,
the race-the-wind, the skiver,
the shag-the-hare, the hedge-squatter,
the dew-hammer, the dew-hopper,
the sit-tight, the grass-bounder,
the jig-foot, the earth-sitter,
the light-foot, the fern-sitter,
the kail-stag, the herb-cropper.

The creep-along, the sitter-still,
the pintail, the ring-the-hill,
the sudden start,
the shake-the-heart,
the belly-white,
the lambs-in-flight.

The gobshite, the gum-sucker,
the scare-the-man, the faith-breaker,
the snuff-the-ground, the baldy skull,
(his chief name is scoundrel.)

The stag sprouting a suede horn,
the creature living in the corn,
the creature bearing all men's scorn,
the creature no one dares to name.'

When you have got all this said
then the hare's strength has been laid.
Then you might go faring forth –

east and west and south and north,
wherever you incline to go –
but only if you're skilful too.
And now, Sir Hare, good-day to you.
God guide you to a how-d'ye-do
with me: come to me dead
in either onion broth or bread.

Seamus Heaney

(1939–2013)

Rabbit

You have no option but to transgress,
being born on the central reservation

of a ring-road, no reason to perceive
the daffodils as a phalanx.

You execute your kite-dance, your paws
are transfixed by something ungiving,

not imprinted on your brain. Your course
is set by your shadow ahead,

you must follow your nostrils
through the city's perfume,

leaping above and below the scent
of diesel, liquorice, fox.

Regina Weinert

Fox

I heard a cough
as if a thief was there
outside my sleep
a sharp intake of air

a fox in her fox-fur
stepping across
the grass in her black gloves
barked at my house

just so abrupt and odd
the way she went
hungrily asking
in the heart's thick accent

in such serious sleepless
trespass she came
a woman with a man's voice
but no name

as if to say: it's midnight
and my life
is laid beneath my children
like gold leaf

Alice Oswald

(1966–)

Pike

Pike, three inches long, perfect
Pike in all parts, green tigering the gold.
Killers from the egg: the malevolent aged grin.
They dance on the surface among the flies.

Or move, stunned by their own grandeur
Over a bed of emerald, silhouette
Of submarine delicacy and horror.
A hundred feet long in their world.

In ponds, under the heat-struck lily pads –
Gloom of their stillness:
Logged on last year's black leaves, watching upwards.
Or hung in an amber cavern of weeds

The jaws' hooked clamp and fangs
Not to be changed at this date;
A life subdued to its instrument;
The gills kneading quietly, and the pectorals.

Three we kept behind glass,
Jungled in weed: three inches, four,
And four and a half: fed fry to them –
Suddenly there were two. Finally one

With a sag belly and the grin it was born with.
And indeed they spare nobody.
Two, six pounds each, over two foot long.
High and dry in the willow-herb –

One jammed past its gills down the other's gullet:
The outside eye stared: as a vice locks –
The same iron in this eye
Though its film shrank in death.

A pond I fished, fifty yards across,
Whose lilies and muscular tench
Had outlasted every visible stone
Of the monastery that planted them –

Stilled legendary depth:
It was as deep as England. It held
Pike too immense to stir, so immense and old
That past nightfall I dared not cast

But silently cast and fished
With the hair frozen on my head
For what might move, for what eye might move.
The still splashes on the dark pond,

Owls hushing the floating woods
Frail on my ear against the dream
Darkness beneath night's darkness had freed,
That rose slowly towards me, watching.

Ted Hughes

(1930–1998)

Mud Shrimp

she swam
only at night
on the spring tides

in the silk light of water
slipping her over
the mud flats

when they studied why she did it
drifted far beyond her limits
though it made her vulnerable
to prey

several theories came
but none swam
at night in a spring tide
in the silk light unsure
of itself
becoming only what is left
after breaking

Elizabeth-Jane Burnett

(1980–)

Song: 'Where the bee sucks, there suck I'

(*from* The Tempest)

Where the bee sucks, there suck I:
In a cowslip's bell I lie;
There I couch when owls do cry.
On the bat's back I do fly
After summer merrily.
Merrily, merrily shall I live now
Under the blossom that hangs on the bough.

William Shakespeare

(1564–1616)

Bees

Here are my bees,
brazen, blurs on paper,
besotted; buzzwords, dancing
their flawless, airy maps.

Been deep, my poet bees,
in the parts of flowers,
in daffodil, thistle, rose, even
the golden lotus; so glide,
gilded, glad, golden, thus –

wise – and know of us:
how your scent pervades
my shadowed, busy heart,
and honey is art.

Carol Ann Duffy

(1955–)

June

I read the fixed wave of a honeycomb page
and notice as I turn it over from recto to verso
how the central O of each empty cell
is imprinted over the X of the one beneath.

This is a palimpsest of hugs and kisses,
a page of the hive broken free when the library fell.
These stacks of vanes that were spoken aloud by bees
are silent now and smell of a dark sweetness.

From the upturned hollow of a willow
a brittle fin of murmuring floats in my hand
its makers blown to the end of their own voices.
O, says the honeycomb: O, O, O.

Charles Bennett

(1954–)

The Birkdale Nightingale

(*Bufo calamito – the Natterjack toad*)

On Spring nights you can hear them
two miles away, calling their mates
to the breeding place, a wet slack in the dunes.
Lovers hiding nearby are surprised
by desperate music. One man searched all night
for a crashed spaceship.

For amphibians, they are terrible swimmers:
where it's tricky to get ashore, they drown.
By day, they sleep in crevices under the boardwalk,
run like lizards from cover to cover
without the sense to leap when a gull snaps.
Yes, he can make himself fearsome,
inflating his lungs to double his size.
But cars on the coast road are not deterred.

She will lay a necklace of pearls in the reeds.
Next morning, a dog will run into the water and scatter them.
Or she'll spawn in a footprint filled with salt rain
that will dry to a crust in two days.

Still, when he calls her and climbs her
they are well designed. The nuptial pads on his thighs
velcro him to her back. She steadies beneath him.

The puddle brims with moonlight.
Everything leads to this.

Jean Sprackland

(1962–)

The World of Birds

Birds fill our countryside, our cities and our consciousness. Their music is nature's soundtrack, their flight patterns make us more aware of the sky and our own place back on the ground, and their nesting behaviours can somehow mirror our own.

There are birds everywhere, and for this collection, there were so many poems to choose from: beautiful paper birds flying down to settle on the page. For poets, birds offer moments of noticing, but are often also metaphors – for people, places, our states of mind, and all the dark and light of natural impulse.

We sit there, breathing, steaming up
The windows and watching

As the heron feints
To a fleck on the line of the lake

(from 'Heron' by Simon Armitage)

The Woods and Banks

The woods and banks of England now,
    Late coppered with dead leaves and old,
Have made the early violets grow,
    And bulge with knots of primrose gold.
Hear how the blackbird flutes away,
    Whose music scorns to sleep at night:
Hear how the cuckoo shouts all day
    For echoes – to the world's delight:
Hullo, you imp of wonder, you –
    Where are you now, cuckoo? Cuckoo?

William Henry Davies

(1871–1940)

A Blackbird Singing

It seems wrong that out of this bird,
Black, bold, a suggestion of dark
Places about it, there yet should come
Such rich music, as though the notes'
Ore were changed to a rare metal
At one touch of that bright bill.

You have heard it often, alone at your desk
In a green April, your mind drawn
Away from its work by sweet disturbance
Of the mild evening outside your room.

A slow singer, but loading each phrase
With history's overtones, love, joy
And grief learned by his dark tribe
In other orchards and passed on
Instinctively as they are now,
But fresh always with new tears.

R.S. Thomas

(1913–2000)

Cuckoo! Cuckoo!

Wading thigh high through wet grasses
    makes me ten years old again
        chewing and spitting sweet stalks –
        hay meadows were forever.

I know this sward like my classmates' register:
    Buttercup, Campion, Lady's Smock...
        Ragged Robin, Rattle, Sorrel.....
        but it's too quiet – only rain whispers.

Now, the first *Cuckoo* cry cracks open friends' smiles.
    I can't hear it but recall is loud   absence
deafening.   Every spring, Mum and I
        competed to claim the earliest cuckoo.

By May hundreds of heard-but-never-seen cuckoos
calling constantly   close by in the tree,
        close up under the eaves,
drove us to echo, 'Shut-up! Shut-up!'

Decades of slow-fade

        silent waiting.

A kerfuffle of crows at the boundary hedge –
        a quick-draw of binoculars from holster

At the centre of the mob, misted lenses
        find a grey blur
focus on down-pointed wings as they fly
        leaving a trace of cuckoo on a mind left behind.

Eyes strain for clearer sighting
                    rubbed out lines of old drafts.

Two notes and faraway things come closer.

Chris Kinsey

(1956–)

To a Swallow Building Under Our Eaves

Thou too hast travelled, little fluttering thing—
Hast seen the world, and now thy weary wing
        Thou too must rest.
But much, my little bird, could'st thou but tell,
I'd give to know why here thou lik'st so well
        To build thy nest.

Thou hast passed fair places in thy flight;
A world lay all beneath thee where to light;
        And, strange thy taste,
Of all the varied scenes that met thine eye—
Of all the spots for building 'neath the sky—
        To choose this waste.

Did fortune try thee? — was thy little purse
Perchance run low, and thou, afraid of worse,
        Felt here secure?
Ah, no! thou need'st not gold, thou happy one!
Thou know'st it not. Of all God's creatures, man
        Alone is poor.

What was it, then? — some mystic turn of thought,
Caught under German eaves, and hither brought,
        Marring thine eye
For the world's loveliness, till thou art grown
A sober thing that does but mope and moan,
        Not knowing why?

Nay, if thy mind be sound, I need not ask,
Since here I see thee working at thy task
     With wing and beak.
A well-laid scheme doth that small head contain,
At which thou work'st, brave bird, with might and main,
     Nor more need'st seek.

In truth, I rather take it thou hast got
By instinct wise much sense about thy lot,
     And hast small care
Whether an Eden or a desert be
Thy home, so thou remain'st alive, and free
     To skim the air.

God speed thee, pretty bird; may thy small nest
With little ones all in good time be blest.
     I love thee much;
For well thou managest that life of thine,
While I — oh, ask not what I do with mine!
     Would I were such!

Jane Welsh Carlyle

(1801–1866)

Nest

to snuggle to coorie doon to snoodle
a half-world of care.

a gowpen of shoogling egg
roofed by warm breast.

a weaving of twigs,
eaves studded with river-mud huts.

a precariousness in wind.
a responsibility of worms, sand eels, gnats.

a rock ledge with fifty thousand screams.
the heart of a hedge.

full stops in winter branches
each a basket of hope.

Char March

(1961–)

Murmuration

The starlings lean
like woodsmoke on the fields,
and blow away.

Bedded in leaves the Wood of Cree
aches in the gale
and sleepwalks into winter.

Rain maps the hills.
Our roaming thoughts
drain down to silt.

Your house is filled with hollow coats.
The mice climb in the walls,
familiar ghosts.

The starlings start to tilt,
they make an end, pull out their stitches,
fold, descend.

Jean Atkin

(1959–)

St Kilda's Wren

I thought you said 'rain'. You said wren,
small haunter of bog and lichen,
loud as gulls' laughter, fierce as men.

Let me guess. Who was St Kilda?
Housewife? Healer? Abbey builder?
Or a man? The rain blows wilder,

on to the railway bank. The bird
flits down, swollen, small brown word.
The male, who wove each nest, is heard

shrilled, triumphant, darts up when
other birds shrink from storm or fen,
shouts to the saintless. Rain, wren, wren.

Alison Brackenbury

(1953–)

The Dipper

It was winter, near freezing,
I'd walked through a forest of firs
when I saw issue out of the waterfall
a solitary bird.

It lit on a damp rock,
and, as water swept stupidly on,
wrung from its own throat
supple, undammable song.

It isn't mine to give.
I can't coax this bird to my hand
that knows the depth of the river
yet sings of it on land.

Kathleen Jamie

(1962–)

Curlew

She dips her bill in the rim of the sea.
Her beak is the ellipse
of a world much smaller
than that far section of the sea's
circumference. A curve enough to calculate
the field's circle and its heart
of eggs in the cold grass.

All day while I scythed my territory
out of nettles, laid claim to my cantref,
she has cut her share of sky. Her song bubbles
long as a plane trail from her savage mouth.
I clean the blade with newspaper. Dusk blurs
circle within circle till there's nothing left
but the egg pulsing in the dark against her ribs.
For each of us the possessed space contracts
to the nest's heat, the blood's small circuit.

Gillian Clarke

(1937–)

Heron

You pull onto the soft verge
And the tyres slacken into the dirt.

I pass the field-glasses
From the glove compartment
And you fumble, finding a focus
Through the action of the wipers

And describe it to me: how it
Hangs in the shallows, shaking the rain
From its featherings. How it watches,
Then cautiously adopts

Its fishing position, then wades
Thoughtfully forward, then holds again.
You go on piecing out the picture
And I affect not to listen

Until you put the glasses down
And I realise you've stopped talking.
We sit there, breathing, steaming up
The windows and watching

As the heron feints
To a fleck on the line of the lake
Like a wood-chip flaw
On slate Ingres paper

And the hilltops are water-marked
If we look hard enough.

Simon Armitage

(1963–)

Choughs at Cape Cornwall

call on one note
      to each another
            across the sky
of Kenidjack and Nanquidno,
      there and back
          and here again,
               wing-fingers spread
as if wind were a plaything,
      as they sidetumble from a height,
          swingrise on the curve
of an updraft, fold their wings,
      freefall downcliff,
      chuffed to tool the gusts
          and perfect the precision
of their landing
      next to one another
          on the same shelf of rock.

Rebecca Gethin

(1953–)

Seabird's Blessing

We are crowds of seabirds,
makers of many angles,
workers that unpick a web
of the air's threads and tangles.

Pray for us when we fight
the wind one to one;
let not that shuddering strength
smash the cross of the wing-bone.

O God the featherer,
lift us if we fall;
preserve the frenzy in our mouths,
the yellow star in the eyeball.

Christ, make smooth the way
of a creature like a spirit
up from its perverse body
without weight or limit.

Holy ghost of heaven,
blow us clear of the world,
give us the utmost of the air
to heave on and to hold.

Pray for us this weird
bare place – we are screaming
O sky count us not as nothing
O sea count us not as nothing

Alice Oswald

(1966–)

The Wild Swans at Coole

The trees are in their autumn beauty,
The woodland paths are dry,
Under the October twilight the water
Mirrors a still sky;
Upon the brimming water among the stones
Are nine-and-fifty swans.

The nineteenth autumn has come upon me
Since I first made my count;
I saw, before I had well finished,
All suddenly mount
And scatter wheeling in great broken rings
Upon their clamorous wings.

I have looked upon those brilliant creatures,
And now my heart is sore.
All's changed since I, hearing at twilight,
The first time on this shore,
The bell-beat of their wings above my head,
Trod with a lighter tread.

Unwearied still, lover by lover,
They paddle in the cold
Companionable streams or climb the air;
Their hearts have not grown old;
Passion or conquest, wander where they will,
Attend upon them still.

But now they drift on the still water,
Mysterious, beautiful;
Among what rushes will they build,
By what lake's edge or pool
Delight men's eyes when I awake some day
To find they have flown away?

William Butler Yeats

(1865–1939)

Autumn Birds

The wild duck startles like a sudden thought,
And heron slow as if it might be caught.
The flopping crows on weary wings go by
And grey beard jackdaws noising as they fly.
The crowds of starnels whizz and hurry by,
And darken like a clod the evening sky.
The larks like thunder rise and suthy round,
Then drop and nestle in the stubble ground.
The wild swan hurries hight and noises loud
With white neck peering to the evening clowd.
The weary rooks to distant woods are gone.
With lengths of tail the magpie winnows on
To neighbouring tree, and leaves the distant crow
While small birds nestle in the edge below.

John Clare

(1793–1864)

The Eagle

He clasps the crag with crooked hands;
Close to the sun in lonely lands,
Ring'd with the azure world, he stands.

The wrinkled sea beneath him crawls;
He watches from his mountain walls,
And like a thunderbolt he falls.

Alfred, Lord Tennyson

(1809–1892)

The Darkling Thrush

I leant upon a coppice gate
    When Frost was spectre-grey,
And Winter's dregs made desolate
    The weakening eye of day.
The tangled bine-stems scored the sky
    Like strings of broken lyres,
And all mankind that haunted nigh
    Had sought their household fires.

The land's sharp features seemed to be
    The Century's corpse outleant,
His crypt the cloudy canopy,
    The wind his death-lament.
The ancient pulse of germ and birth
    Was shrunken hard and dry,
And every spirit upon earth
    Seemed fervourless as I.

At once a voice arose among
    The bleak twigs overhead
In a full-hearted evensong
    Of joy illimited;
An aged thrush, frail, gaunt, and small,
    In blast-beruffled plume,
Had chosen thus to fling his soul
    Upon the growing gloom.

So little cause for carolings
    Of such ecstatic sound
Was written on terrestrial things
    Afar or nigh around,
That I could think there trembled through

His happy good-night air
Some blessed Hope, whereof he knew
   And I was unaware.

Thomas Hardy

(1840–1928)

Hawk Roosting

I sit in the top of the wood, my eyes closed.
Inaction, no falsifying dream
Between my hooked head and hooked feet:
Or in sleep rehearse perfect kills and eat.

The convenience of the high trees!
The air's buoyancy and the sun's ray
Are of advantage to me;
And the earth's face upward for my inspection.

My feet are locked upon the rough bark.
It took the whole of Creation
To produce my foot, my each feather:
Now I hold Creation in my foot

Or fly up, and revolve it all slowly –
I kill where I please because it is all mine.
There is no sophistry in my body:
My manners are tearing off heads –

The allotment of death.
For the one path of my flight is direct
Through the bones of the living.
No arguments assert my right:

The sun is behind me.
Nothing has changed since I began.
My eye has permitted no change.
I am going to keep things like this.

Ted Hughes

(1930–1998)

from To a Skylark

Hail to thee, blithe Spirit!
Bird thou never wert,
That from Heaven, or near it,|
Pourest thy full heart
In profuse strains of unpremeditated art.

Higher still and higher
From the earth thou springest
Like a cloud of fire;
The blue deep thou wingest,
And singing still dost soar, and soaring ever singest.

In the golden lightning
Of the sunken sun,
O'er which clouds are bright'ning,
Thou dost float and run;
Like an unbodied joy whose race is just begun.

The pale purple even
Melts around thy flight;
Like a star of Heaven,
In the broad day-light
Thou art unseen, but yet I hear thy shrill delight.

Teach me half the gladness
That thy brain must know,
Such harmonious madness
From my lips would flow
The world should listen then, as I am listening now.

Percy Bysshe Shelley

(1792–1822)

Bird Walk

White nights feather my mind.
I am a giant of sleeplessness, as high
as the cliff where auks lay teetering eggs
which droop roughly, like tears.

They won't roll. My mind rolls.
To sleep, I must think like the birds
in camouflage, decoys and patrols.

Redshanks storm the grass, post sentries
on telegraph poles, as highly strung
as the oystercatchers all in a flap,
outcrying their young to mislead crows
who shrug and brag and lunge.

At three a.m., a black cormorant dives.
A needle, a nightfall, it closes my eyes.

Lavinia Greenlaw

(1962–)

Nightjar

Listen to the nightjar, hear her holy tremblings –
star litter, night fragment, slip down a spine of grass.
A circumstance of sound electrifies the heath,
opens up the dark. Though she's dead now,
or to all effects, in silence, gone
like a ghost ship rising, you can hear her.
Her voice is both inside you
and around you. She pushes you away,
she asks you to be near.
In the stillness, let the sound debris, in wild track,
moth-like, poke the dust. Put your finger on the space
she finds in you, her rattle notes, her love rambles:
let her open up a space, beside you – there
now, there – close beside your heart.

Deryn Rees-Jones

(1968–)

The Way Through the Woods

These poems take us on a journey through the woods – stopping to look down at the snowdrops, mushrooms and lichens, as well as up into the canopy. Trees, and their attendant flora and fauna, are perhaps some of the best measures of the health of our wild places.

Philip Larkin's lines *The trees are coming into leaf / Like something almost being said* beautifully sum up our imaginative connection to the emerging trees, grasses and flowers. For Larkin, and for us, *they almost seem to say / Begin afresh, afresh, afresh* – a call for their renewal and for ours. So often in these poems, there is the metaphor of the flora speaking and us listening. As Emily Berry writes in her poem 'Canopy', *I think they were telling us to survive.*

something is moving
up through the dark and down through the dark

(from 'Oak' by Katharine Towers)

To a Snowdrop

Lone Flower, hemmed in with snows and white as they
But hardier far, once more I see thee bend
Thy forehead, as if fearful to offend,
Like an unbidden guest. Though day by day,
Storms, sallying from the mountain-tops, waylay
The rising sun, and on the plains descend;
Yet art thou welcome, welcome as a friend
Whose zeal outruns his promise! Blue-eyed May
Shall soon behold this border thickly set
With bright jonquils, their odours lavishing
On the soft west-wind and his frolic peers;
Nor will I then thy modest grace forget,
Chaste Snowdrop, venturous harbinger of Spring,
And pensive monitor of fleeting years!

William Wordsworth

(1770–1850)

'Loveliest of trees, the cherry now'

(*from* A Shropshire Lad)

Loveliest of trees, the cherry now
Is hung with bloom along the bough,
And stands about the woodland ride
Wearing white for Eastertide.

Now, of my threescore years and ten,
Twenty will not come again,
And take from seventy springs a score,
It only leaves me fifty more.

And since to look at things in bloom
Fifty springs are little room,
About the woodlands I will go
To see the cherry hung with snow.

A.E. Housman

(1859–1936)

I Wandered Lonely as a Cloud

I wandered lonely as a cloud
That floats on high o'er vales and hills,
When all at once I saw a crowd,
A host, of golden daffodils;
Beside the lake, beneath the trees,
Fluttering and dancing in the breeze.

Continuous as the stars that shine
And twinkle on the milky way,
They stretched in never-ending line
Along the margin of a bay:
Ten thousand saw I at a glance,
Tossing their heads in sprightly dance.

The waves beside them danced; but they
Out-did the sparkling waves in glee:
A poet could not but be gay,
In such a jocund company:
I gazed—and gazed—but little thought
What wealth the show to me had brought:

For oft, when on my couch I lie
In vacant or in pensive mood,
They flash upon that inward eye
Which is the bliss of solitude;
And then my heart with pleasure fills,
And dances with the daffodils.

William Wordsworth

(1770–1850)

Elderflower

Spilling your bridal whites over the churchyard wall,
slipping them off into my hand,
dusting my wrist with powder –
elixir of musk and honey, blanc de blancs –

I take you for a sign, just when I need one
along the lane, in the maze of lanes
with their dense hedges, ditches hidden under leaves,
the blind bend, the owl and the speeding van.

The rachis flushed with pink where it divides,
the panicle a host of new stars,
a few still closed in their silken nibs,
white glowing with green in the long June dusk.

Token of freshness, growing out of silence –
grant me remission, a truce with the past.
Make everything possible, here, now
in this clean state of erasure. I ask

not to start again, but to lose my way
down the steep track in the deepening dark
and to find instead this common-or-garden grace.
To break you and carry you with me as a torch.

Jean Sprackland

(1962–)

July

When I think of the rare fen violet
whose seeds can wait for decades for just
the right kind of disturbance,

whose bluish-white petals
have crept into sight again after forty years,
I remember Sedge Fen Drove

where lesser spearwort steps across
the queasy ooze of ground I am sinking into,
and I come again to the place

where I see how the names of plants
are thoughts in the fertile mind of Wicken Fen,
and how you have to wait sometimes

for the right kind of disturbance
before you can blossom, and then at last
you remember the rare fen violet.

Charles Bennett

(1954–)

The Trees

The trees are coming into leaf
Like something almost being said;
The recent buds relax and spread,
Their greenness is a kind of grief.

Is it that they are born again
And we grow old? No, they die too,
Their yearly trick of looking new
Is written down in rings of grain.

Yet still the unresting castles thresh
In fullgrown thickness every May.
Last year is dead, they seem to say,
Begin afresh, afresh, afresh.

Philip Larkin

(1922–1985)

Binsey Poplars

felled 1879

My aspens dear, whose airy cages quelled,
   Quelled or quenched in leaves the leaping sun,
  All felled, felled, are all felled;
     Of a fresh and following folded rank
         Not spared, not one
         That dandled a sandalled
     Shadow that swam or sank
On meadow & river & wind-wandering weed-winding bank.

O if we but knew what we do
      When we delve or hew —
Hack and rack the growing green!
     Since country is so tender
To touch, her being só slender,
That, like this sleek and seeing ball
But a prick will make no eye at all,
Where we, even where we mean
        To mend her we end her,
    When we hew or delve:
After-comers cannot guess the beauty been.
   Ten or twelve, only ten or twelve
     Strokes of havoc unselve
       The sweet especial scene,
    Rural scene, a rural scene,
    Sweet especial rural scene.

Gerard Manley Hopkins

(1844–1889)

from Oak

after a mast year
an inkling like
the thought of a thought

far from the green skits of the wood
an escapee acorn
can't contain itself

lacking something that's upwards
and something that's downwards
though neither knows what is lacked

(they'll know when they get to it)

no need for this broken old suitcase
which has been stepped out of
like a magician's box is stepped out of

something is moving
up through the dark and down through the dark
with a creaking you wouldn't believe how loud

surely it must hurt
tiny white wavering frond
tiny quivering foot

it's tempting to ask what if
Wind had not rattled so hard at the tree
Jay had not been called away across the field
Rain had not softened the blows
Earth had not agreed to pocket
this one for keeps

tiny white wavering frond
tiny quivering foot

wend your way lightwards
wend your way darkwards

Katharine Towers

(1961–)

Canopy

The weather was inside.

The branches trembled over the grass as if to
apologise; then they thumped and they came in.

And the trees shook everything off until they were
bare and clean. They held on to the ground with
their long feet and leant into the gale and back again.

This was their way with the wind.

They flung us down and flailed above us with their
visions and their pale tree light.

I think they were telling us to survive. That's what a leaf feels
like anyway. We lay under their great awry display and they
tattooed us with light.

They got inside us and made us speak; I said my first
word in their language: 'canopy'.

I was crying and it felt like I was feeding. Be my
mother, I said to the trees, in the language of trees,
which can't be transcribed, and they shook their hair
back, and they bent low with their many arms, and
they looked into my eyes as only trees can look into
the eyes of a person, they touched me with the rain on
their fingers till I was all droplets, till I was mist, and
they said they would.

Emily Berry

(1981–)

The Greenwood

A nice idea, but no one is going to take to it
to escape the law, and what it offers isn't
a country of itself, complete with courts and fools.

There may be barbed wire and tracks made by
heavy plant hauling timber down to yards. There may
be sign-posted rights of way for all abilities.

The Greenwood isn't what it used to be. But stand me
in a still, cold-folded clearing and I will see shades
of the old world, the commonwealth of trees.

Jonathan Davidson

(1964–)

The Way Through the Woods

They shut the road through the woods
    Seventy years ago.
Weather and rain have undone it again,
    And now you would never know
There was once a road through the woods
    Before they planted the trees.
It is underneath the coppice and heath,
    And the thin anemones.
    Only the keeper sees
That, where the ring-dove broods,
    And the badgers roll at ease,
There was once a road through the woods.

Yet, if you enter the woods
    Of a summer evening late,
When the night-air cools on the trout-ringed pools
    Where the otter whistles his mate,
(They fear not men in the woods,
    Because they see so few.)
You will hear the beat of a horse's feet,
    And the swish of a skirt in the dew,
    Steadily cantering through
The misty solitudes,
    As though they perfectly knew
    The old lost road through the woods.
But there is no road through the woods.

Rudyard Kipling

(1865–1936)

Among the Great Oaks in Autumn

among the oaks
my skin is a type of bark

I give birth to rocks
the same thing that happens

to me happens to them
a leaf will flutter down

my roots and into another world
turning to ghosts

creeping back as the light goes low
I am painted dancers sprouting

from the vines
the strings of my body vibrate

to the strings of the rain

Jason Allen-Paisant

(1980–)

Lichen

Who listens
like lichen listens

assiduous millions of black
and golden ears?

You hear

       and remember

but I'm speaking
to the lichen.

The little ears prunk,
scorch and blacken.

The little golden
mouths gape.

Jen Hadfield

(1978–)

Mushrooms

Overnight, very
Whitely, discreetly,
Very quietly

Our toes, our noses
Take hold on the loam,
Acquire the air.

Nobody sees us,
Stops us, betrays us;
The small grains make room.

Soft fists insist on
Heaving the needles,
The leafy bedding,

Even the paving.
Our hammers, our rams,
Earless and eyeless,

Perfectly voiceless,
Widen the crannies,
Shoulder through holes. We

Diet on water,
On crumbs of shadow,
Bland-mannered, asking

Little or nothing.
So many of us!
So many of us!

We are shelves, we are
Tables, we are meek,
We are edible,

Nudgers and shovers
In spite of ourselves.
Our kind multiplies:

We shall by morning
Inherit the earth.
Our foot's in the door.

Sylvia Plath

(1932–1963)

The Other World of Water

In these poems, we follow some of our beautiful UK rivers – from their mysterious source, with the water diviners of Jonathan Davidson's poem, to tumbling Welsh waterfalls from Vernon Watkins, and through the saltmarsh to the scribbled margins of the sea. Here are some much-loved poems of the sea, as well as some new voices.

I must go down to the seas again, for the call of the morning tide
Is a wild call, and a clear call that may not be denied.

(from 'Sea-Fever' by John Masefield)

The Water Diviners

We, unexpectedly chosen,
gripping the thin branch,
twig even, in our soft hands,
to walk the rough field
divining the saint's well
or the spring – lost since the fall
of the water table, since the rise
of the Severn Trent Authority.

We are a boy and a girl.
And watching us, confused
as we should be but are not,
that short, energetic dog,
his tail twitching,
his wet note tasting
the salt of the country.

And beneath us
the other world of water,
working where the loam
gives into fleshy clay
or demarcates
the skeletal chalk,
to surface a mile away
in a vapour of midges
or never to surface.

Jonathan Davidson

(1964–)

Water Colours

The trembling water glimpsed through dark tangle
Of late-month April's delicatest thorn,
One moment put the cuckoo-flower to scorn
Where its head hangs by sedges, Severn bank-full.
But dark water has a hundred fires on it;
As the sky changes it changes and ranges through
Sky colours and thorn colours, and more would do,
Were not the blossom truth so quick on it,
And beauty brief in action as first dew.

Ivor Gurney

(1890–1937)

Waterfalls

Always in that valley in Wales I hear the noise
   Of waters falling.
                    There is a clump of trees
  We climbed for nuts; and high in the trees the boys
    Lost in the rookery's cries
         Would cross, and branches cracking under their knees

Would break, and make in the winter wood new gaps.
  The leafmould covering the ground was almost black,
     But speckled and striped were the nuts we threw in our caps,
     Milked from split shells and cups,
        Secret as chestnuts when they are tipped from a sack,

Glossy and new.
          Always in that valley in Wales
I hear that sound, those voices. They keep fresh
  What ripens, falls, drops into darkness, fails,
    Gone when dawn shines on scales,
        And glides from village memory, slips through the mesh,

And is not, when we come again.
             I look:
  Voices are under the bridge, and that voice calls,
    Now late, and answers,
             then, as the light twigs break
    Back, there is only the brook reminding the stones
             where, under a breath, it falls.

Vernon Watkins

(1906–1967)

from **Dart**

by the bridge, an eel watcher

(two places I've seen eels, bright whips of flow
like stopper waves the rivercurve slides through
trampling around at first you just make out
the elver movement of the running sunlight
three foot under the road-judder you hold
and breathe contracted to an eye-quiet world
while an old dandelion unpicks her shawl
and one by one the small spent oak flowers fall
then gently lift a branch brown tag and fur
on every stone and straw and drifting burr
when like a streamer from your own eye's iris
a kingfisher spurts through the bridge whose axis
is endlessly in motion as each wave
photos its flowing to the bridge's curve
if you can keep your foothold, snooping down
then suddenly two eels let go get thrown
tumbling away downstream looping and linking
another time we scooped a net through sinking
silt and gold and caught one strong as bike-chain
stared for a while then let it back again
I never pass that place and not make time
to see if there's an eel come up the stream
I let time go as slow as moss, I stand
and try to get the dragonflies to land
their gypsy-coloured engines on my hand)

Alice Oswald

(1966–)

Severn Song

(for John Karl Gross)

The Severn was brown and the Severn was blue –
not this-then-that, not either-or,
no mixture. Two things can be true.
The hills were clouds and the mist was a shore.

The Severn was water, the water was mud
whose eddies stood and did not fill,
the kind of water that's thicker than blood.
The river was flowing, the flowing was still,

the tide-rip the sound of dry fluttering wings
with waves that did not break or fall.
We were two of the world's small particular things.
We were old, we were young, we were no age at all,

for a moment not doing, nor coming undone –
words gained, words lost, till who's to say
which was the father, which was the son,
a week, or fifty years, away.

But the water said *earth* and the water said *sky*.
We were everyone we'd ever been or would be,
every angle of light that says *You*, that says *I*,
and the sea was the river, the river the sea.

Philip Gross

(1952–)

Saltmarsh and Skylark

A man sits in a bowl of sunlight on the saltmarsh, clearly alone.
A slight hollow brings shelter on this husky threshing floor,
Stamped out flat by heavy, working weather.

The marshes are etched by veins of water so salt
It rustles faintly as it flows; sequin platelets buffed bright by acid –
So salt it iceburns, with the stick and pull of skin on frosted metal.

The water is carding its knotty white strings slowly
Through the blue brown fish-flesh of the mud.
Slowly laces and unlaces the filaments in the corridor of gills.

The marsh is a scribble of tough whip-grass and matted vetch;
Cross-hatched collage of God's leftovers;
Odd peelings from the plughole, pilled tweed
And steel wool, glued on in tufts by a nervous understudy.

Dry brown curves of grass, bowing down in pools of white light;
A crumbling-rusk-in-skimmed-milk landscape.
The man squints upwards into larksong and closes his eyes.

As he tilts, he inhales the song all the warm way up the light.
The eyelids thinly filter, impressing into hot blood-orange,
Then melting crabshell, embossed in pink and greening bronze;

Strange bunching and wellings, expansive dissolution;
The matt black stamen of the skylark's turning tongue,
The brain-stem's softly-bound bouquet of pulses.

Katherine Pierpoint

(1961–)

Sea-Fever

I must go down to the seas again, to the lonely sea and the sky,
And all I ask is a tall ship and a star to steer her by;
And the wheel's kick and the wind's song and the white sail's shaking,
And a grey mist on the sea's face, and a grey dawn breaking.

I must go down to the seas again, for the call of the running tide
Is a wild call and a clear call that may not be denied;
And all I ask is a windy day with the white clouds flying,
And the flung spray and the blown spume, and the sea-gulls crying.

I must go down to the seas again, to the vagrant gypsy life,
To the gull's way and the whale's way where the wind's like a whetted knife;
And all I ask is a merry yarn from a laughing fellow-rover,
And quiet sleep and a sweet dream when the long trick's over.

John Masefield

(1878–1967)

Painted Ladies

Although she would never normally set foot
Beyond the railway line, because the beach is dirty,
Her Mam said; spoilt before she was born, rust-stained and orange,

Black with slag and dolly-wash, its terrible lagoons
Haemorrhaging sulphates, oxides – some ancient outrage
No one alive can remember now – Leanne sets out

Down her grandda's red-black raa' – path of putter and hewer,
Backshift, foreshift; pigeon-cree; policeman and picket –
With his bairn in a Tupperware box. Up the White Lea lane,

Through fireweed and meadow grass, she wades, to the brink –
To the windy cliff at Shippersea, the clean horizon.
In a handful of ashes she brings her Mam to beauty.

Then far below, incarnadine, ochre, black, white
Pigments of caustic pools and residues, fly up, combine –
Embers, aflame inside, aglow in the grate,

Flickering from knapweed to thistle-top, they rise
Blazing before her – butterflies – the fields
From Hawthorn Hive to Eden Dene on fire with them.

Katrina Porteous

(1960–)

from Once More the Sea

As soon as I am folded in, I breathe out and relax. The forest
suits dull weather, damp tinted green-and-grey, ringing eyes with
wakefulness.

At the base runs the burn, tucked beside wide, palm-shaped leaves.
They might be wild rhubarb, but I don't always know the names. I
just cross the dene-mouth briefly, following the coastal path.

On my way out, I pass a chorus of hello! orange flowers like strings
of dripped jewels, their colour a deep lit eye. I will find their
name later and they turn out to be *Montbretia*, an African species
brought to English gardens in 1880. They'd escape to wildlands by
1911. And through

> the arch of the towering
> red-brick Viaduct,
> I am back at sea. Brown butterflies
> frisk my hair

Phoebe Power

(1993–)

The Tide Rises, the Tide Falls

The tide rises, the tide falls,
The twilight darkens, the curlew calls;
Along the sea-sands damp and brown
The traveller hastens toward the town,
 And the tide rises, the tide falls.

Darkness settles on roofs and walls,
But the sea, the sea in the darkness calls;
The little waves, with their soft, white hands,
Efface the footprints in the sands,
 And the tide rises, the tide falls.

The morning breaks; the steeds in their stalls
Stamp and neigh, as the hostler calls;
The day returns, but nevermore
Returns the traveller to the shore,
 And the tide rises, the tide falls.

Henry Wadsworth Longfellow

(1807–1882)

By the Sea

Why does the sea moan evermore?
   Shut out from heaven it makes its moan,
It frets against the boundary shore;
    All earth's full rivers cannot fill
    The sea, that drinking thirsteth still.

Sheer miracles of loveliness
   Lie hid in its unlooked-on bed:
Anemones, salt, passionless,
    Blow flower-like; just enough alive
    To blow and multiply and thrive.

Shells quaint with curve, or spot, or spike,
   Encrusted live things argus-eyed,
All fair alike, yet all unlike,
    Are born without a pang, and die
    Without a pang, and so pass by.

Christina Rossetti

(1830–1894)

Carne

The sand is strewn with sea-weed shapes
that gently move with tide's continual sway –
inscrutable, like Japanese calligraphy.
Rock-pools fill and swirl, then drain,
then fill again each day.
Baby crabs lie upside down in sand,
salt-spattered by the spray.
No sound, no sound at all, but solitary high gull-cry,
the rush and wash of waves on shingle, stone and scree.
Ocean is too big a word to use, too large a thing to see.
My eye moves out from this secluded bay
to a horizon that is much too far away.
No sight, no sight at all this way
but blue on blue on blue and a vague distant thread of grey.
My thoughts will not stay still –
how restlessly they divigate and splay.
I am dwarfed, humbled, chastened, scattered –
even by this little slip of sea.

Lucy Newlyn

(1956–)

First Light at Porth Ust

at daybreak the land
flicks open the book
of itself the rocks
an ancient text

two seagulls scribble
through the greyness
spelling out
the first gleam of light

as light opens pages
of sky and stone
choughs write themselves in
and out

surf sweeps over
the pebbles and rocks
scrabbles and scours
all hollows and crevices

tides have fettled every joint
and hollow in boulders
a carpentry of water and rock
fitting rock like knuckles and knees

water in niches and cracks
puts seaflesh on stone
chisellling it
into the shape of cove

sea water feeds beadlet
and snakelock anemones,
soft as eye balls
but gripping barnacle-tight

Rebecca Gethin

(1953–)

Daed-traa

I go to the rockpool at the slack of the tide
to mind me what my poetry's for.

It has its ventricles, just like us –
pumping brine, like bull's blood, a syrupy flow.

It has its theatre –
hushed and plush.

It has its Little Shop of Horrors.
It has its crossed and dotted monsters.

It has its cross-eyed beetling Lear.
It has its billowing Monroe.

I go to the rockpool at the slack of the tide
to mind me what my poetry's for.

For monks, it has barnacles
to sweep the broth as it flows, with fans,
grooming every cubic millimetre.

It has its ebb, the easy heft of wrack from rock,
like plastered, feverish locks of hair.

It has its *flodd*.
It has its welling god
with puddled, podgy cheeks and jaw.

It has its holy hiccup.

Its minute's silence

         daed–traa.

I go to the rockpool at the slack of the tide
to mind me what my poetry's for.

Jen Hadfield

(1978–)

Dover Beach

The sea is calm tonight.
The tide is full, the moon lies fair
Upon the straits; on the French coast the light
Gleams and is gone; the cliffs of England stand,
Glimmering and vast, out in the tranquil bay.
Come to the window, sweet is the night-air!
Only, from the long line of spray
Where the sea meets the moon-blanched land,
Listen! you hear the grating roar
Of pebbles which the waves draw back, and fling,
At their return, up the high strand,
Begin, and cease, and then again begin,
With tremulous cadence slow, and bring
The eternal note of sadness in.

Sophocles long ago
Heard it on the Ægean, and it brought
Into his mind the turbid ebb and flow
Of human misery; we
Find also in the sound a thought,
Hearing it by this distant northern sea.

The Sea of Faith
Was once, too, at the full, and round earth's shore
Lay like the folds of a bright girdle furled.
But now I only hear
Its melancholy, long, withdrawing roar,
Retreating, to the breath
Of the night-wind, down the vast edges drear
And naked shingles of the world.

Ah, love, let us be true
To one another! for the world, which seems
To lie before us like a land of dreams,
So various, so beautiful, so new,
Hath really neither joy, nor love, nor light,
Nor certitude, nor peace, nor help for pain;
And we are here as on a darkling plain
Swept with confused alarms of struggle and flight,
Where ignorant armies clash by night.

Matthew Arnold

(1822–1888)

Fianuis

Well, friend, we're here again —
        sauntering the last half-mile to the land's frayed end
to find what's laid on for us, strewn across the turf—
gull feathers, bleached shells,
                     a whole bull seal, bone-dry,
knackered from the rut
(we knock on his leathern head, but no one's home).

Change, change — that's what the terns scream
                  down at their seaward rocks;
fleet clouds and salt kiss—
everything else is provisional,
               us and all our works.
I guess that's why we like it here:
          Listen — a brief lull,
              a rock pipit's seed-small notes.

Kathleen Jamie

(1962–)

Night-Piece

Now independent, beautiful and proud,
Out of the vanishing body of a cloud
Like its arisen soul the full moon swims
Over the sea, into whose distant brims
Has flowed the last of the light. I am alone.
Even the diving gannet now is flown
From these unpeopled sands. A mist lies cold
Upon the muffled boundaries of the world.
The lovely earth whose silence is so deep
Is folded up in night, but not in sleep.

Eleanor Farjeon

(1881–1965)

Moors, Heaths and Mountains

The idea of the wildness of nature as metaphor for the poet is threaded through these poems. In this chapter, nature is held up as a mirror that reflects the emotions; we range across the map – from the heaths and moorlands, over the hills, to the mountains of the mind.

to strike a balance between known and not,
between the dogged journey and the rest

(from 'Hilles, Edge' by Glyn Maxwell)

Landscape and I

Landscape and I get on together well.
Though I'm the talkative one, still he can tell
His symptoms of being to me, the way a shell
Murmurs of oceans.

Loch Rannoch lapses dimpling in the sun.
Its hieroglyphs of light fade one by one
But re-create themselves, their message done,
For ever and ever.

That sprinkling lark jerked upward in the blue
Will daze to nowhere but leave himself in true
Translation – hear his song cascading through
His disappearance.

The hawk knows all about it, shaking there
An empty glove on steep chutes of the air
Till his yellow foot cramps on a squeal, to tear
Smooth fur, smooth feather.

This means, of course, Schiehallion in my mind
Is more than mountain. In it he leaves behind
A meaning, an idea, like a hind
Couched in a corrie.

So then I'll woo the mountain till I know
The meaning of the meaning, no less. Oh,
There's a Schiehallion anywhere you go.
The thing is, climb it.

Norman MacCaig

(1910–1996)

On Allt yr Esgair

Under the serpent galaxy
    the motifs of stone hills recur
in scoops and curls across the sky
    cutting the landscape's signature.

Under the rhythms of the name
    the coiling water of the Usk
inscribes red rock and combs red clay
    with a gleaming mercury arabesque.

And the larval micromoth
    inside the thickness of a leaf
mines a tunnel with her mouth
    to carve a curious hieroglyph.

What else is left for us but this?
    With pen and brush to shape our track,
like moths and streams and hills and stars,
    a human shadow on the rock.

Christopher Meredith

(1955–)

Hilles, Edge

A man has clambered up a hill so high
five counties hold their breath. There the air there is
is all his own and however far away
are farms and rivers they can all hear this.

He breathes again, his call unechoed. Winds
are pestering him with nothing. Soon enough
he takes a quarter-turn to look askance
and fixedly along the ridge, as if

to strike a balance between known and not,
between the dogged journey and the rest,
acknowledging the endlessness not yet,
scanning the close-at-hand for interest,

or at least a place to crouch in out of the wind
while the others scramble up. They will see in him
the mark of having seen. He will see in them
the awe he can now only understand.

Glyn Maxwell

(1962–)

My Heart's in the Highlands

My heart's in the Highlands, my heart is not here,
My heart's in the Highlands, a-chasing the deer;
Chasing the wild-deer, and following the roe,
My heart's in the Highlands, wherever I go.

Farewell to the Highlands, farewell to the North,
The birth-place of Valour, the country of Worth;
Wherever I wander, wherever I rove,
The hills of the Highlands for ever I love.

Farewell to the mountains, high-cover'd with snow,
Farewell to the straths and green vallies below;
Farewell to the forests and wild-hanging woods,
Farewell to the torrents and loud-pouring floods.

My heart's in the Highlands, my heart is not here,
My heart's in the Highlands, a-chasing the deer;
Chasing the wild-deer, and following the roe,
My heart's in the Highlands, wherever I go.

Robert Burns

(1759–1796)

from **Loud without the wind was roaring**

Loud without the wind was roaring
Through th'autumnal sky;
Drenching wet, the cold rain pouring,
Spoke of winter nigh.
All too like that dreary eve,
Did my exiled spirit grieve.
Grieved at first, but grieved not long,
Sweet—how softly sweet!—it came;
Wild words of an ancient song,
Undefined, without a name.

For the moors! For the moors, where the short grass
Like velvet beneath us should lie!
For the moors! For the moors, where each high pass
Rose sunny against the clear sky!

For the moors, where the linnet was trilling
Its song on the old granite stone;
Where the lark, the wild sky-lark, was filling
Every breast with delight like its own!

What language can utter the feeling
Which rose, when in exile afar,
On the brow of a lonely hill kneeling,
I saw the brown heath growing there?

It was scattered and stunted, and told me
That soon even that would be gone:
It whispered, 'The grim walls enfold me,
I have bloomed in my last summer's sun.'

But not the loved music, whose waking
Makes the soul of the Swiss die away,
Has a spell more adored and heartbreaking
Than, for me, in that blighted heath lay.

Well—well; the sad minutes are moving,
Though loaded with trouble and pain;
And some time the loved and the loving
Shall meet on the mountains again!

Emily Brontë

(1818–1848)

Wuthering Heights

The horizons ring me like faggots,
Tilted and disparate, and always unstable.
Touched by a match, they might warm me,
And their fine lines singe
The air to orange
Before the distances they pin evaporate,
Weighting the pale sky with a solider color.
But they only dissolve and dissolve
Like a series of promises, as I step forward.

There is no life higher than the grasstops
Or the hearts of sheep, and the wind
Pours by like destiny, bending
Everything in one direction.
I can feel it trying
To funnel my heat away.
If I pay the roots of the heather
Too close attention, they will invite me
To whiten my bones among them.

The sheep know where they are,
Browsing in their dirty wool-clouds,
Grey as the weather.
The black slots of their pupils take me in.
It is like being mailed into space,
A thin, silly message.
They stand about in grandmotherly disguise,
All wig curls and yellow teeth
And hard, marbly baas.

I come to wheel ruts, and water
Limpid as the solitudes
That flee through my fingers.
Hollow doorsteps go from grass to grass;
Lintel and sill have unhinged themselves.
Of people the air only
Remembers a few odd syllables.
It rehearses them moaningly:
Black stone, black stone.

The sky leans on me, me, the one upright
Among the horizontals.
The grass is beating its head distractedly.
It is too delicate
For a life in such company;
Darkness terrifies it.
Now, in valleys narrow
And black as purses, the house lights
Gleam like small change.

Sylvia Plath

(1932–1963)

'Only some spires...'

Only some spires of bright green grass
Transparently in sunshine quivering.

Emily Brontë

(1818–1848)

High Summer on a Shropshire Hill

Cocksfoot, crested dog's tail, Yorkshire fog,
Common bent, Brown bent, Italian rye grass –
sown way back, to improve the ley. Wavy hair-grass,
fine fescues, soft rushes, bromes whose awns irritate
animal palates. Wefts of herbs: sorrels, bedstraws,
mouse ear, hawkbit, eyebright, tormentil, vanishing
flowers: yellow rattle which tells when to cut hay,
slow-growing harebells – dying on verges from nitrous
exhaust, knapweeds, speedwells, trefoils, timothy,
yellow oat grass, sweet vernal grass, all names and niches,
rhizomes and runners, all paraphernalia of panicles, ligules,
shoots, sheaths, spikelets and glumes. All waving grace
and grain – millions of years' resilience to cutting and cropping.
Famine waits as we taint soils, strain genes, skew climate.

Chris Kinsey

(1956–)

The Healing of Little Woolden Moss

Little Woolden Moss SJ68869546

There's beauty in what is repaired,
in old wrongs softened
in moss, and all of its colours.

Though not everything can be restored
here there are dragonflies
and their wings are bright windows –

they lift you.
Here, healing is still in progress
and it sounds like summer.

It is skylark and curlew, buzzard –
the wide sky
where all things are possible,

and the earth
which holds its stories within it
and tells them through curve and ditch

because this a place of purpose
where hard work unmakes mistakes
and though the ground is unstable,

it is soft,
and a man will stand here for hours
to name the birds

and where once there were wounds,
there are scars
and they shimmer

and in summer
the swifts and the swallows return.

Clare Shaw

(1972–)

Bog

Kneeling for marshfruit like spilled
Beads bedded in displaying moss
I notice a licked frog dragging
His drenched fatigues up and through
The barring spears and stalks of orange
Bog asphodel as if in terror
Of unknown purposes, as though
I were a weight of sky, a whole
Universe of beak and gullet,
And not, as I am, a mere slider
And stumbler like him, damp to the hips,
Reaching for tussocks, scrabbling for almost
Nothing: these little speckled fruits,
Chill marbles of a forgotten tourney,
Aching playthings of a lost garden
That has always been mostly water,
A place of utter loneliness,
Terrain of the asphodel and of the frog.

John Fuller

(1937–)

High Waving Heather

High waving heather, 'neath stormy blasts bending,
Midnight and moonlight and bright shining stars;
Darkness and glory rejoicingly blending,
Earth rising to heaven and heaven descending,
Man's spirit away from its drear dongeon sending,
Bursting the fetters and breaking the bars.

All down the mountain sides, wild forest lending
One mighty voice to the life-giving wind;
Rivers their banks in the jubilee rending,
Fast through the valleys a reckless course wending,
Wider and deeper their waters extending,
Leaving a desolate desert behind.

Shining and lowering and swelling and dying,
Changing for ever from midnight to noon;
Roaring like thunder, like soft music sighing,
Shadows on shadows advancing and flying,
Lightning-bright flashes the deep gloom defying,
Coming as swiftly and fading as soon.

Emily Brontë

(1818–1848)

Our Place in Nature

The poems in this final section deal directly with our conversation with nature, and its effect upon us, both good and bad. They question and criticise our impact on the natural world and, finally, ask us to make peace with it.

come, take pleasure in turns and overgrowths
get closer to the land: you are a part
of this world, not separate or distinct

(from 'The Path of Grass' by Dan Simpson)

The year's at the spring

(*from* Pippa Passes)

The year's at the spring
And day's at the morn;
Morning's at seven;
The hillside's dew-pearled;
The lark's on the wing;
The snail's on the thorn:
God's in His heaven—
All's right with the world!

Robert Browning

(1812–1889)

In the Fields

Lord when I look at lovely things which pass,
Under old trees the shadow of young leaves
Dancing to please the wind along the grass,
Or the gold stillness of the August sun on the August sheaves;
Can I believe there is a heavenlier world than this?
And if there is
Will the heart of any everlasting thing
Bring me these dreams that take my breath away?
They come at evening with the home-flying rooks and the scent
of hay,
Over the fields. They come in spring.

Charlotte Mew

(1869–1928)

from Lines Written a Few Miles Above Tintern Abbey

And all its aching joys are now no more,
And all its dizzy raptures. Not for this
Faint I, nor mourn nor murmur; other gifts
Have followed; for such loss, I would believe,
Abundant recompense. For I have learned
To look on nature, not as in the hour
Of thoughtless youth; but hearing oftentimes
The still sad music of humanity,
Nor harsh nor grating, though of ample power
To chasten and subdue.—And I have felt
A presence that disturbs me with the joy
Of elevated thoughts; a sense sublime
Of something far more deeply interfused,
Whose dwelling is the light of setting suns,
And the round ocean and the living air,
And the blue sky, and in the mind of man

William Wordsworth

(1770–1850)

To Nature

It may indeed be fantasy, when I
Essay to draw from all created things
Deep, heartfelt, inward joy that closely clings;
And trace in leaves and flowers that round me lie
Lessons of love and earnest piety.
So let it be; and if the wide world rings
In mock of this belief, it brings
Nor fear, nor grief, nor vain perplexity.
So will I build my altar in the fields,
And the blue sky my fretted dome shall be,
And the sweet fragrance that the wild flower yields,
Shall be the incense I will yield to Thee,
Thee only God! and thou shalt not despise
Even me, the priest of this poor sacrifice.

Samuel Taylor Coleridge

(1772–1834)

The Lake Isle of Innisfree

I will arise and go now, and go to Innisfree,
And a small cabin build there, of clay and wattles made;
Nine bean rows will I have there, a hive for the honey-bee,
And live alone in the bee-loud glade.

And I shall have some peace there, for peace comes dropping slow,
Dropping from the veils of the morning to where the cricket sings;
There midnight's all a-glimmer, and noon a purple glow,
And evening full of the linnet's wings.

I will arise and go now, for always night and day
I hear lake water lapping with low sounds by the shore;
While I stand on the roadway, or on the pavements grey,
I hear it in the deep heart's core.

William Butler Yeats

(1865–1939)

Naming

Some time in my middle years
I needed to know the names of things.
For so many years I walked this path
in the woods before I knew these leaves
as dog's mercury or that white star
as wood anemone.

      It is as if the naming
of things will slow the earth's spin,
fix my feet to the ground.
I tell myself as I walk,
that is mallow, vetch, viper's bugloss;
a smoky bracket fungus on the fallen
paper birch. This delicate shell
a heath snail, that high keening
a sparrow hawk.

      The seasons are harder
to name; is this spring, or the beginning
of summer? I will know
      when winter comes.

Angela France

(1955–)

Charismatic Animals

Is it cheaper to weep for a sea otter – clutching
paws in the water – than a lake? The scientist
herself is moved by ospreys. The poet
is guilty of magical thinking, reads
each tip of the barn owl's head as a message,
each heron as gift, each slow worm, each bee
as a personal envoy. Her neighbours. But the lake
is a grandmother. She has her own charisma.
She hides galaxies in her core with her gilly heart
as huge and as heavy as a moon.

Polly Atkin

(1980–)

When Birds Nest

I can't bear it when birds nest
on the angle of a door that might
at any minute close,
or in the pocket of a coat,
hung to dry in a shed
or a lawnmower shell, so close
to utter destruction.

Why trust us with the delicate brood?
We come to the earth with blood
on our hands: with our pesticides
and herbicides, our nets
thrown over hedges,
the way we block owl holes,
the echo of gunshot never far away.

We do, say the blackbirds
on the garden fence. *Us*
say the martins under the eaves.
Birds, the wren says, bringing us down
to her letter-box nest so we
can hear the world turning too.

Wendy Pratt

(1978–)

The force that through the green fuse drives the flower

The force that through the green fuse drives the flower
Drives my green age; that blasts the roots of trees
Is my destroyer.
And I am dumb to tell the crooked rose
My youth is bent by the same wintry fever.

The force that drives the water through the rocks
Drives my red blood; that dries the mouthing streams
Turns mine to wax.
And I am dumb to mouth unto my veins
How at the mountain spring the same mouth sucks.

The hand that whirls the water in the pool
Stirs the quicksand; that ropes the blowing wind
Hauls my shroud sail.
And I am dumb to tell the hanging man
How of my clay is made the hangman's lime.

The lips of time leech to the fountain head;
Love drips and gathers, but the fallen blood
Shall calm her sores.
And I am dumb to tell a weather's wind
How time has ticked a heaven round the stars.

And I am dumb to tell the lover's tomb
How at my sheet goes the same crooked worm.

Dylan Thomas

(1914–1953)

Ariel

Where the bee sucks,
neonicotinoid insecticides
in a cowslip's bell lie,
in fields purple with lavender,
yellow with rape,
and on the sunflower's upturned face;
on land monotonous with cereals and grain,
merrily,
        merrily;
sour in the soil,
sheathing the seed, systemic
in the plants and crops,
the million acres to be ploughed,
seething in the orchards now,
under the blossom
                that hangs
on the bough.

Carol Ann Duffy

(1955–)

Spring, An Inventory

On 20 March 2021, the National Trust, in partnership with the Arts and Humanities Research Council, invited members of the public to contribute to a new piece of poetry by sharing their observations of the arrival of spring. The poem by Elizabeth-Jane Burnett weaves together the responses of the 400 participants, the numbers reflecting the frequency of the words appearing across the submissions.

Fifty-four hopes in the hardwood held,
slow, the hour brightens
through damp roots and fused shoots the pressure wells,
fifty-one blossoms on the cherry swell,
tiny beech leaves ripen.
Fifty-four hopes in the hardwood held
slow, the hour brightens.

Forty-four trees in the waking woods,
forty-one spilling gardens.
Five cherry trees where the blackbirds stood,
thirty-five joys through their gleaming broods,
thirty-eight buds nectar-guarding
in forty-four trees in the waking woods,
in forty-one spilling gardens.

Thirty-four lights in the dark wood spots,
thirty greens, fizzily fruiting
thirty-five suns in the speckled moss,
three daylights, four pink lights blush the docks,
twenty-two bees new-moving –
thirty-four lights in the dark wood spots,
thirty greens, fizzily fruiting.

Twenty-eight songs sing eleven blackbirds,
twenty-three mornings in chorus.
Sixteen skies, six skylarks stirred,
Five rains, four wrens, two herons surge,
four bluebells, two curlews, two horses.
Twenty-eight songs sing eleven blackbirds
Twenty-three mornings in chorus.

One moon and one mouth, one sea and one star,
only one cuckoo, one car.
One silence of engines and suddenly choirs
in the grass, in the soil, on the branch.
Four hundred notes singing out of one bar,
four hundred lungs breathing one fresh start,
one moon and one mouth, one sea and one star,
only one cuckoo, one car.

Elizabeth-Jane Burnett

(1980–)

There Will Come Soft Rains

There will come soft rains and the smell of the ground,
And swallows circling with their shimmering sound;

And frogs in the pools singing at night,
And wild plum trees in tremulous white,

Robins will wear their feathery fire
Whistling their whims on a low fence-wire;

And not one will know of the war, not one
Will care at last when it is done.

Not one would mind, neither bird nor tree
If mankind perished utterly;

And Spring herself, when she woke at dawn,
Would scarcely know that we were gone.

Sara Teasdale

(1884–1933)

The Path of Grass

Take my hand, my love, and let us wander
along this path of grass as if it was
made just for us – feet and bodies carry
our sprits along gently, through soft scent
and let us be content in wild Nature
allow a childlike wonder to infuse
your thoughts, which – freshly renewed – can expand
beyond the paths of man, that stone laid down
untamed ground made strangely straight and measured
come, take pleasure in turns and overgrowths
get closer to the land: you are a part
of this world, not separate or distinct
do not pass by leaf, root, branch or petal
revel in nature: take the path of grass.

Dan Simpson

(1985–)

Domicilium

It faces west, and round the back and sides
High beeches, bending, hang a veil of boughs,
And sweep against the roof. Wild honeysucks
Climb on the walls, and seem to sprout a wish
(If we may fancy wish of trees and plants)
To overtop the apple trees hard-by.

Red roses, lilacs, variegated box
Are there in plenty, and such hardy flowers
As flourish best untrained. Adjoining these
Are herbs and esculents; and farther still
A field; then cottages with trees, and last
The distant hills and sky.

Behind, the scene is wilder. Heath and furze
Are everything that seems to grow and thrive
Upon the uneven ground. A stunted thorn
Stands here and there, indeed; and from a pit
An oak uprises, Springing from a seed
Dropped by some bird a hundred years ago.

In days bygone—
Long gone—my father's mother, who is now
Blest with the blest, would take me out to walk.
At such a time I once inquired of her
How looked the spot when first she settled here.
The answer I remember. 'Fifty years
Have passed since then, my child, and change has marked
The face of all things. Yonder garden-plots
And orchards were uncultivated slopes
O'ergrown with bramble bushes, furze and thorn:

That road a narrow path shut in by ferns,
Which, almost trees, obscured the passers-by.

Our house stood quite alone, and those tall firs
And beeches were not planted. Snakes and efts
Swarmed in the summer days, and nightly bats
Would fly about our bedrooms. Heathcroppers
Lived on the hills, and were our only friends;
So wild it was when we first settled here.'

Thomas Hardy

(1840–1928)

The Ditch

*I usd to drop down behind a hedge bush or dyke and write down
my things upon the crown of my hat*

As John Clare rises from the ditch where he writes,
frogs bob up through duckweed and roll their eyelids.
The poet's coat and hat, they thought, *were rain-clouds.*
The scribbling pen and riffling paper: they were the rain.
The cloud and rain have moved like lovers out of sight.
Woodlice wake under bark. Nests nudge from within.
Buds are easter-hedged with eggs. A world unwinds
unwinding a world: hedges are easter-egged with buds;
woodlice wake under nests; bark nudges from within;
the lovers and rain move like clouds out of sight;
a scribbling paper and riffling rain: they are the pen;
a thought's hat and coat and rain-cloud: they are poets;
frogs roll up through duckweed and bob their eyelids.
And John Clare settles down by a ditch, where he writes.

David Morley

(1964–)

Stargazing

The night is fine and dry. It falls and spreads
the cold sky with a million opposites
that, for a spell, seem like a million souls
and soon, none, and then, for what seems a long time,
one. Then of course it spins. What is better to do
than string out over the infinite dead spaces
the ancient beasts and spearmen of the human
mind, and if not the real ones, new ones?

But, try making them clear to one you love,
(whoever is standing by you is one you love
when pinioned by the stars): you will find it quite
impossible, but like her more for thinking
she sees that constellation.
After the wave of pain, you will turn to her
and, in an instant, change the universe
to a sky you were glad you came out to see.

This is the act of the descended gods
of every age and creed: to weary of all
that never ends, to take a human hand
and go back into the house.

Glyn Maxwell

(1962–)

Notes

Charles Bennett, 'June' (p. 49) and 'July' (p. 85)

These poems are from a series of twelve that reflect the course of a year at Wicken Fen during Charles Bennett's residency there in 2014. Wicken Fen is the National Trust's oldest nature reserve and one of Europe's most important wetlands, home to more than 9,000 species across its flowering meadows, sedge and reedbeds. The endangered fen violet had been spotted there again that year for the first time in a decade. Wicken Fen Vision, launched in 1999, is an ambitious plan to form a diverse landscape for wildlife and people that stretches from Wicken Fen to the edge of Cambridge. Grazing herds of Highland cattle and Konik ponies are helping to create a range of new habitats across the reserve.

Jane Welsh Carlyle, 'To a Swallow Building Under Our Eaves' (p. 58)

Jane Welsh Carlyle was a prolific letter-writer, and she produced much of her poetry and prose in the context of her correspondences. None of her work was published during her lifetime. Born Jane Baillie Welsh in 1801, she married the writer Thomas Carlyle in 1826. It was during their time at Craigenputtock, a remote farm in Dumfriesshire, that she wrote this poem. In 1834, the Carlyles moved to a house in Cheyne Row in Chelsea – now Carlyle House, and in the care of the National Trust.

Thomas Hardy, 'The Darkling Thrush' (p. 72)

This poem was published in 1900, by which point Thomas Hardy was living at Max Gate – a home he had designed with close attention to, and inspiration from, its natural surroundings. Visitors to Max Gate today can see the large windows in Hardy's study, without mullions and transoms, that allow a clear view of the garden. Hardy would walk daily in his garden and regularly in the countryside beyond, taking the route from Max Gate to Hardy's Cottage weekly in his later life. The influence of the Dorset landscape is felt powerfully throughout his writing.

William Wordsworth, 'To a Snowdrop' (p. 80)

Visitors to Wordsworth House in Cockermouth, Cumbria can imagine a young William Wordsworth playing in the riverside garden and roaming the surrounding countryside with his sister, Dorothy. It was there, during those early years, that William first learned his deep appreciation for the natural world – one that would so greatly inspire his poetry.

William Wordsworth, 'I Wandered Lonely as a Cloud' (p. 82)

On 15 April 1802, William and Dorothy Wordsworth walked round Ullswater. In Dorothy's diary entry for that day, she described the multitude of daffodils that they had encountered there by the water. These would have been wild daffodils, or Lent lilies, with nodding heads and pale yellow outer petals. Conservation work by the National Trust at Ullswater means that walkers can still enjoy an array of these wild flowers each spring, just as William and Dorothy once did.

Rudyard Kipling, 'The Way Through the Woods' (p. 92)

Rudyard Kipling moved with his family to Bateman's, East Sussex, in 1902, and he lived there for the rest of his life. Bateman's, a seventeenth-century manor house, is surrounded by the fields and woodlands of the High Weald countryside, with the River Dudwell flowing through the valley. This landscape provided inspiration for many of Kipling's stories and poems. Some of the paths around Bateman's are grown over, now, but visitors can still walk some of the same routes that Kipling would have known.

**Katrina Porteous, 'Painted Ladies'
(p. 107); Phoebe Power, extract from
'Once More the Sea' (p. 108)**

The 11-mile stretch from Seaham to
Hartlepool on the Durham Coast, now an
Area of Outstanding Natural Beauty, was
once the site of some of the county's deep
coal mines. A massive clean-up project
in the 1990s began a transformation of
the landscape that is still ongoing. In
the summer of 2019, Katrina Porteous
and Phoebe Power undertook writing
residencies on the Durham Coast as part of
the National Trust's 'People's Landscapes'
project. They were asked to reflect on the
area's changing landscape and explore
the perspectives of its communities. In
partnership with New Writing North, their
work was commissioned for the Durham
Book Festival.

Lucy Newlyn, 'Carne' (p. 111)

Nestled in a secluded bay on Cornwall's
Roseland Peninsula, Carne beach is in the
care of the National Trust. At low tide, it
forms one long, glorious stretch of sand
with its neighbouring Pendower beach.

Matthew Arnold, 'Dover Beach' (p. 116)

The White Cliffs of Dover form an iconic
landmark that has been a powerful symbol
of hope and home for centuries. On a clear
day, the clifftops provide breathtaking views
that stretch across the Channel to France.
The National Trust now looks after the
White Cliffs, helping to protect the chalk
grassland and the many species that make it
their home.

**Samuel Taylor Coleridge,
'To Nature' (p. 139)**

In 1797, Samuel Taylor Coleridge moved
his young family from Bristol to what
is now known as Coleridge Cottage, in
Nether Stowey, Somerset. In desperate
search of calm and inspiration, he wanted
to 'wander like a breeze' in the Quantock
Hills. The three years Coleridge spent in

Nether Stowey were certainly creatively
productive; he wrote some of his best-
known works there and he collaborated
with William Wordsworth to produce the
seminal Romantic work *Lyrical Ballads*. The
period helped to shape Coleridge's poetic
vision and it would echo through his later
work, including this poem written c. 1820.

**Dan Simpson,
'The Path of Grass' (p. 149)**

Lancelot 'Capability' Brown designed the
Grecian Valley at Stowe during his time as
head gardener there. It is a fine example
of his talent for designing naturalistic
landscapes that blended seamlessly with
their surrounding countryside. In 2019,
the National Trust commissioned Dan
Simpson to write a response to the Grecian
Valley, reflecting on the eighteenth-century
pastoral idyll. This extract is from 'Under
the Hawthorn'.

Thomas Hardy, 'Domicilium' (p. 150)

'Hardy's Cottage', in Higher
Brockhampton, Dorset, was built by the
poet's grandfather in around 1800. The
small thatch and cob cottage, with its
idyllic garden, sits quietly in the shadow of
ancient and wildlife-rich woodland. Just
beyond it is an area of heather and gorse,
or furze, known as Black Heath. Thomas
Hardy was born and raised at the cottage.
Influenced by the environment of his rural
upbringing, he was deeply attuned to
the natural world and the significance of
setting. He wrote this poem at the cottage
as a teenager. Visitors to Hardy's Cottage
today can recognise the same atmosphere
that the poet describes in 'Domicilium'; it
is a place harmoniously intertwined with
its surroundings, where human experience
and imagination are shaped by the presence
of nature.

Index of Poets

Index of Poems

Acknowledgements

'Among the Great Oaks in Autumn' by Jason Allen-Paisant is reproduced by kind permission of Carcanet Press Limited. 'April' by Jean Sprackland is reproduced by kind permission of Penguin Random House. 'April Rise' by Laurie Lee is reproduced by kind permission of Peters Fraser + Dunlop on behalf of the Estate of Laurie Lee. 'Ariel' by Carol Ann Duffy is reproduced by kind permission of RCW. 'Bees' by Carol Ann Duffy is reproduced by kind permission of RCW. 'Bird Walk' by Lavinia Greenlaw is reproduced by kind permission of Faber. 'The Birkdale Nightingale' by Jean Sprackland is reproduced by kind permission of Penguin Random House. 'A Blackbird Singing' by R.S. Thomas is reproduced by kind permission of Orion Publishing Group Limited. 'Bog' by John Fuller is reproduced by kind permission of Penguin Random House. 'Brown Hare' by Clare Shaw, which was funded by the Great Manchester Wetlands, Carbon Landscape Partnership and the National Lottery Heritage Fund and commissioned by Manchester Literature Festival and Lancashire Wildlife Trust in 2021, is reproduced by kind permission of the author. 'Canopy' by Emily Berry is reproduced by kind permission of Faber. 'Carne' by Lucy Newlyn (lucynewlyn.com) is reproduced by kind permission of the author. 'Charismatic Animals' by Polly Atkin is reproduced by kind permission of Seren Books. 'Choughs at Cape Cornwall' by Rebecca Gethin, first published in *Foxglove Journal* in 2020, is reproduced by kind permission of the author. 'Considering the Snail' by Thom Gunn is reproduced by kind permission of Faber. 'Cuckoo! Cuckoo!' by Chris Kinsey, first published in *From Rowan Ridge* (Fair Acre Press, 2019), is reproduced by kind permission of the author. 'Curlew' by Gillian Clarke is reproduced by kind permission of Carcanet Press Limited. 'Daed-traa' by Jen Hadfield is reproduced by kind permission of Bloodaxe Books. 'Dart' by Alice Oswald is reproduced by kind permission of Faber. 'The Dipper' by Kathleen Jamie is reproduced by kind permission of Pan Macmillan. 'The Ditch' by David Morley is reproduced by kind permission of the author. 'Elderflower' by Jean Sprackland is reproduced by kind permission of Penguin Random House. 'February on Reservoir Hill' by Chris Kinsey, first published in *From Rowan Ridge* (Fair Acre Press, 2019) is reproduced by kind permission of the author. 'Fianuis' by Kathleen Jamie is reproduced by kind permission of Pan Macmillan. 'First Light at Porth Ust' by Rebecca Gethin is reproduced by kind permission of the author. 'The force that through the green fuse drives the flower' by Dylan Thomas is reproduced by kind permission of David Higham Associates. 'Fox' by Alice Oswald is reproduced by kind permission of Penguin Random House. 'The Greenwood' by Jonathan Davidson, first published in *The Tree Line* (Worple Press, 2017), is reproduced by kind permission of the author. 'Hawk Roosting' by Ted Hughes is reproduced by kind permission of Faber. 'The Healing of Little Woolden Moss' by Clare Shaw, which was funded by the Great Manchester Wetlands, Carbon Landscape Partnership and the National Lottery Heritage Fund and commissioned by Manchester Literature Festival and Lancashire Wildlife Trust in 2021, is reproduced by kind permission of the author. 'Heron' by Simon Armitage is reproduced by kind permission of Faber. 'High Summer on a Shropshire Hill' by Chris Kinsey, first published in *From Rowan Ridge* (Fair Acre Press, 2019), is reproduced by kind permission of the author. 'Hilles, Edge' by Glyn Maxwell is reproduced by kind permission of Micheline Steinberg Associates. 'Hunting the Stag' by Polly Atkin is reproduced by kind permission of Seren Books. 'July' by Charles Bennett, first published in *Cloud River* (Cinnamon Press, 2019), is reproduced by kind permission of the author. 'June' by Charles Bennett, first published in *Cloud River* (Cinnamon Press, 2019), is reproduced by kind permission of the author. 'Landscape and I' by Norman MacCaig is reproduced by kind permission of Birlinn Ltd. 'Lichen' by Jen Hadfield is reproduced by kind permission of Bloodaxe Books. 'Looking Down On Glen Canisp' by Norman MacCaig is reproduced by kind permission of Birlinn Ltd. 'Mud Shrimp' by Elizabeth-Jane Burnett is reproduced by kind permission of Penned in the Margins. 'Murmuration' by Jean Atkin, first published in *Full Stops in Winter Branches* (Valley Press, 2018), is reproduced by kind permission of the author. 'Mushrooms' by Sylvia Plath is reproduced by kind permission of Faber. 'The Names of the Hare' by Seamus Heaney is reproduced by kind permission of Faber. 'Naming' by Angela France, first published in *The Hill* (Nine Arches Press, 2017), is reproduced by kind permission of the author. 'Nest' by Char March, first published in *Full Stops in Winter Branches* (Valley Press, 2018), is reproduced by kind permission of the author. 'Nightjar' by Deryn Rees-Jones is reproduced by kind permission of Seren Books. 'Night-Piece' by Eleanor Farjeon is reproduced by kind permission of David Higham Associates. 'Oak' by Katharine Towers is reproduced by kind permission of Pan Macmillan. 'On Allt yr Esgair' by Christopher Meredith is reproduced by kind permission of Seren Books. 'On the First Day of Autumn' by Jason Allen-Paisant is reproduced by kind permission of Carcanet Press Limited. 'Once More the Sea' by Phoebe Power is reproduced by kind permission of the author. 'Painted Ladies' by Katrina Porteous is reproduced by kind permission of the author. 'The Path of Grass' by Dan Simpson is reproduced by kind permission of the author. 'Pike' by Ted Hughes is reproduced by kind permission of Faber. 'Rabbit' by Regina Weinert, which was first published in *Spelt Magazine* in 2021, is reproduced by kind permission of the author. 'St Kilda's Wren' by Alison Brackenbury is reproduced by kind permission of Carcanet Press Limited. 'Saltmarsh and Skylark' by Katherine Pierpoint is reproduced by kind permission of Faber. 'Seabird's Blessing' by Alice Oswald is reproduced by kind permission of Faber. 'Sea-Fever' by John Masefield is reproduced by kind permission of The Society of Authors. 'Severn Song' by Philip Gross is reproduced by kind permission of Bloodaxe Books. 'Spring, An Inventory' by Elizabeth-Jane Burnett is reproduced by kind permission of Curtis Brown. 'Stargazing' by Glyn Maxwell is reproduced by kind permission of Pan Macmillan. 'The Trees' by Philip Larkin is reproduced by kind permission of Faber. 'The Unlooked-for Season' by Jenny Joseph is reproduced by kind permission of Johnson & Alcock Ltd. 'The Water Diviners' by Jonathan Davidson, first published in *A Commonplace – Apples, Bricks and Other People's Poems* (Smith|Doorstop, 2020), is reproduced by kind permission of the author. 'When Birds Nest' by Wendy Pratt is reproduced by kind permission of the author. 'Wrack of Summer' by Polly Atkin is reproduced by kind permission of Seren Books. 'Wuthering Heights' by Sylvia Plath is reproduced by kind permission of Faber. 'The Year's Midnight' by Gillian Clarke is reproduced by kind permission of Carcanet Press Limited.